Hungry Animals

My First Look at a Food Chain

Written by Pamela Hickman
Illustrated by Heather Collins

Kids Can Press Ltd.
Toronto

This is the field
where Jill plays.

This is the wildflower
that grows in the field
where Jill plays.

This is the snake
that swallowed the toad,
that gobbled the bug,
that fed on the wildflower,
that grows in the field
where Jill plays.

This is the owl

that caught the snake,

that swallowed the toad,

that gobbled the bug,

that fed on the wildflower,

that grows in the field

where Jill plays.

These are the owlets

that were fed by the owl,

that caught the snake,

that swallowed the toad,

that gobbled the bug,

that fed on the wildflower,

that grows in the field

where Jill plays.

All gone!